MW00463034

Grow Through

What You

Go Through!

Devotional

Encouragement

for the times

when life happens.

(1 Corinthians 10:13)

(2 Corinthians 12:9)

Written by

Fred Famble

Dedication:

This writing is dedicated to my first-born child GaBrielle! Shauntee, you have taught me how to turn life's setbacks into stepping stones. Never doubt your value and worth! I am proud of you and all that you have accomplished! You are an amazing Christian lady, wife and mother. You set the standard for your sister and brother!

Love Always!

Dad

Let us then with confidence draw near to the throne of grace, that we may receive mercy and find grace to help in time of need. Hebrews 4:16

Publications

"Help in Time of Need" Devotionals

We would love to hear from you!

Follow us on Facebook:
https://www.facebook.com/HTNDevotionals/

Send us an email:
htnbooks@gmail.com

© 2018

All rights reserved. No part of this publication may be reproduced, stored in a retrieval system, or transmitted in any form or by any means-for example electronic photocopy, recording-without the prior written permission of the author. The only exception is brief quotations in printed reviews.

Table of Contents

Introduction

We all have pain points in life that we can think back to. You remember the time that something happened to you that rocked you to your very emotional core! Loss of a job, loss of a spouse, infidelity, or the death of a child or close loved one? That thing that made your moral compass spin out of control and tested (or is testing) every fiber of your mental, physical and spiritual resolve! That event that happened to you that caused time to stop! You did not eat as you should have eaten. Restful sleep eluded you! You played the recording of that pain repeatedly in your mind until you may have made yourself physically sick! Well-meaning friends came by in their futile attempts to offer words of comfort. However, those words never seemed to bridge the emotional canyon deep within your soul!

For some, your pain point may have been physical. While others may have experienced an emotionally painful setback. The purpose of this writing is not to invite you to a pity party. Neither is the purpose of this writing to catalog pain in an effort to affirm one person's pain any greater or less than another. The purpose of this writing is to encourage you (from the word of God) to grow beyond your current pain. To muster up enough physical strength and emotional fortitude to not allow the pain of your circumstance (be it past or present), to become the cement that will encase you and keep you emotionally entombed for the rest of your life! The purpose of this writing is to encourage you like this, "Don't let your current condition become your life-long conclusion!"

You may not realize it right now (especially if you are still trying to navigate your way through your current storm) but God still loves and cares for you! And while it might be hard to fathom at this moment, I remind you that as believers, we must take comfort from His word (no matter what our current situation might be.)

"His divine power has granted to us all things that pertain to life and godliness, through the knowledge of him who called us to his own glory and excellence."
2 Peter 2:3(ESV)

Be assured that God is not playing sick games with you (although at times it may feel like it!) God has not left you neither has He abandoned you! I assure you my reading friend; God's love for you is just as real now as it was before the initial splash of your current pain began. However, the waters at this level of pain that you are wading through are anything but calm and soothing right now. They are boisterous and turbulent! The enemy (to weaken or destroy your faith) is continually stirring them hoping to cause you to give up so that you will "curse God and die" (Job 2:8,9).

My encouragement to you, my friend, during this time of faith testing, is do not give in to the temptation to quit! My prayer for you is the same prayer our Lord offered on Peter's behalf (when Christ foretold of Peters denial):

"Simon, Simon, behold, Satan demanded to have you that he might sift you like wheat, but I have prayed for you that your faith may not fail. And when you have turned again, strengthen your brothers."
Luke 22:31,32 (ESV)

Christ knew and saw in Peter a great accomplishment yet to be done. Our Lord did not deny Peter's current situation of the enemy's real presence and impending goal...*"to have you*

and sift you like wheat!" Instead, Christ chose to proactively speak life, input hope and give spiritual marching orders for the future. *"And when you have turned again, strengthen your brothers."*

My friend, whatever the storm that you are currently weathering, I would like to ask your permission, to walk alongside you for a bit! I would like your permission to provide my shoulder for you to lean on. I would like to walk with you through this rough episode only until you can stand on your own and see the light at the end of the path. Before you ask, the answer is, "No, I'm not a professional counselor or therapist." Then what qualifies me to pen this writing? You may ask? I am just a man who has weathered a few storms. I am a person who can now look back and see certain patterns that helped me and now I will pass those along to you! Remember, the scriptures are a collection of stories about ordinary men who accomplished extraordinary deeds empowered by God! I guess (as Jesus told Peter), "my faith did not fail. I have turned again" (or been converted as the King James Version states) and now my task is to strengthen you!

Before we begin, I would like to ask a few things of you. If the weight of the current (or past) pain you are dealing with has you paralyzed to the point that you cannot remember the last time you had a meal, please, please go eat something. The journey ahead will require all of the physical strength you have. If, the pain of your plight has caused you to cocoon or isolate yourself in one room or area of your home, please get up and move to another room. This change of venue is exactly what you need to get started!

Years ago when I hired a personal trainer to help me start with an exercise program, we began with basic exercises. Each day, we worked a different muscle group (even before I mastered the routines.) When I asked the trainer, why we didn't stick with one thing until I got the hang of it, she taught me a powerful lesson. She said that if we wanted to achieve maximum results, we needed to keep my body in a state of confusion. If I wanted to build muscle mass, I needed to keep up the strength resistance training but never allow my body to get used to one set of exercises!

I have learned that people (like a muscle in weight training), only benefit from the resistance we embrace. "Embracing the resistance stimulates the growth." (Keith Craft) You are about to go through spiritual resistance training! The full benefits and blessings will become more obvious to you at the end of our journey. Before we start, let's pray:

Our heavenly Father, I pray Your blessing on the reader as we begin this faith walk down a path to turn tears into cheers! Help this time that we spend together reflecting on experiences and reading Your word to be pleasing and acceptable in Your sight O Lord our rock and our Redeemer. In the mighty name of Jesus I pray, AMEN!

Now, let's begin...

Chapter One-
You Are Not Alone

Growing up as the oldest sibling (and the only boy in my family) most certainly had its advantages. Very early in my life, I realized that as my father's only son, being male had its freedoms. However, with that "freedom" also came some very real consequences. To say that I was one of those children that were "risk takers" and that I pushed the envelope of parental boundaries would be a bit of an understatement! According to my mother and my grandmother, I was a "handful."

One of my earliest lessons about following directions was one Saturday when I was with my family shopping downtown. There was a department store called, F. W. Wool Worth. My parents had given me strict and implicit instructions before entering the establishment! In short, I was told, "Don't touch nothin... don't ask for nothin... cause you ain't gettin nothing! Stay close to us and in plain sight! Do you understand?" Understanding those orders, I nodded my affirmative and we went into the store. Well, it did not take long for my friends, the store mannequins, to lure me away from my parents. Before long, the fun of going in between the clothes racks playing hide and seek with the mannequins was replaced by sheer terror! They were just gone! I was lost and afraid!

While my heart was pounding and racing, I did what I had seen my parents do countless times. The lady at the register always told my parents to "come back and see me if you need anything else." I took a deep breath (even though I was afraid) went and said, "Excuse me! I need help finding my parents!" She took me by the hand and we began to walk the store looking for my parents. We didn't get too far from her register when we saw my dad around the corner. My dad thanked the nice lady for helping me and she went back to her area. "Dad, I'm sorry I got lost," I said with my heart still racing. I should have listened and done what you said. "Junior, you did good. I was watching around the corner the entire time." You were really never alone.

It would later take years for me to forgive my father for what I thought was a very cruel joke. However, I have come to realize what he did was really for my own good. From that point forward,

I learned my lesson and was more obedient to his instructions. In hindsight, I was able to push past my fear and pain (in the moment) to get the help I needed. I acted on faith in the midst of pain and fear.

That life lesson is also where I recommend you begin my reading, friend. Right now, you may be in the midst of pain. It really doesn't matter (at this point) how you got here (either something you did or something that may have been done that affects you). The real fact is we have to acknowledge and deal with the pain. If you are still traveling down your highway of pain, you have no doubt come past several mile markers that just keep pointing you back to the source of your pain. That is normal. You will have good days and not-so-good days. The important thing here is to realize that you are never alone. Consider 1 Corinthians 10:13 (ESV-English Standard Version):

"No temptation has overtaken you that is not common to man. God is faithful, and he will not let you be tempted beyond your ability, but with the temptation he will also provide the way of escape, that you may be able to endure it."

Consider also 2 Corinthians 12:9,10 (ESV):

But he said to me, "My grace is sufficient

for you, for my power is made perfect in weakness." Therefore, I will boast all the more gladly of my weaknesses, so that the power of Christ may rest upon me. For the sake of Christ, then, I am content with weaknesses, insults, hardships, persecutions, and calamities. For when I am weak, then I am strong.

The author, C.S. Lewis, has this to say about pain:

"Pain insists upon being attended to. God whispers to us in our pleasures, speaks in our consciences, but shouts in our pains. It is His megaphone to rouse a deaf world."

In the Old Testament, the character, Job, provides wonderful insight about how to deliberately choose faith in the midst of suffering. Job is a wealthy man living in a land called Uz with his large family and extensive flocks. He is "blameless" and "upright," always careful to avoid doing evil (1:1). One day, Satan appears before God in heaven. God boasts to Satan about Job's goodness, but Satan argues that Job is only good because God has blessed him abundantly (1:9). Satan challenges God that, if given permission to punish the man, Job will turn and curse God (1:10). God allows Satan to torment Job to test this bold claim, but He forbids Satan to take Job's life in the process.

In the course of one day, Job receives four messages, each bearing separate news that his livestock, servants, and ten children have all died due to marauding invaders or natural catastrophes. Job tears his clothes and shaves his head in mourning, but he still blesses God in his prayers. Satan appears in heaven again, and God grants him another chance to test Job. This time, Job is afflicted with horrible skin sores. His wife encourages him to curse God and to give up and die, but Job refuses, struggling to accept his circumstances.[1] The real point of confirmation and encouragement for me is found in Job 1:21,22:

"And he said, "Naked I came from my mother's womb, and naked shall I return. The LORD gave, and the LORD has taken away; blessed be the name of the LORD." In all this Job did not sin or charge God with wrong."

If we really are going to grow through what we go through, it seems that the first step is to have the proper mindset. Job is the example here by showing that a true and right relationship with God isn't predicated on things! The possessions (including children) were loaned to us by God. We are merely the stewards (or managers) of these blessings entrusted to us. In short, God can do with His stuff, what He well pleases! That is the reason that verse 22, is so affirming and so encouraging, *"in all this Job did not sin or charge God with wrong."*

Notice here that Job never attempted to hide, deny or get around his pain. He tore his clothes, shaved his head, fell on the ground and worshipped God. This first step may in fact be the most difficult. Our natural tendency (especially when in pain) is to want the why questions answered. The book of Job is the perfect example of remaining faithful to God even when we don't have (or get) the answers we seek. As time goes on, the why becomes less important. Choosing faith in the midst of pain will remind you that God is in control.[2]

Chapter Two –
Obey the Signs

It's still one of the most vivid memories I have from my childhood! Even now at age 57, (when I think about it), the feelings of powerlessness and shame try to take over my thoughts. I can still feel the cold from being soaking wet, even though it was a hot Georgia summer afternoon. I can still hear the people laughing. Although most of the faces are blurred in my memory, I do remember some of the faces of the children in the crowd. Faces that would tell their version of this story to the rest of the third grade class tomorrow. Stephanie Winters (whom I knew since the first grade) was there with her family. Timothy Powell (who always picked me first for dodge ball because he said I was the fastest in the class) and his dad. Out of the corner of my eye, I caught a glimpse of the boatman laughing as he was talking with the lifeguard who pulled us out of the water. I still remember the words...forever burned onto my mind (more than the heat of the Georgia summer sun that day). "Them people..." he said. "Them people couldn't read a sign if it was big as the Empire State building..." Their laughter continued. I remember him from the many times that we had come to the lake before. He was a large white man who wore a hat like the Skipper on Gilligan's Island and always had half a cigar in his mouth – never lit though. "I did read the sign," I mumbled very carefully and almost inaudibly under my breath. "I did read the sign but it didn't do no good...he didn't listen to me!" I continued my silent rebellion. I was careful not to be heard. In the late 60's not only was it considered "sassing" to talk back to adults but these were white adults whose idea of civil rights meant to be extra nice to each other.

The fact of the matter was, I did read the sign and told my dad what it said. As we were heading down the paddleboat ramp to get into one of the paddleboats, I read him the sign "Boat Ramp Closed – All Boats Not in Service." Not only was this posted on the pole leading down to the boat ramp, but it was also the same sign that we found in the boat that he (my dad) suggested we take. As I look back on it, I don't know which hurt worse - the fact that he was intoxicated (which was nothing new) or the fact that my father didn't listen to me. At any rate, I remember trusting my dad, ignoring the signs, and getting into the paddleboat.

As we pushed off from the dock, my dad said (as he had many times before), "No matter what you do, junior, keep peddling and we will be alright. With those reassuring words, I did as I was instructed. Within minutes, the paddleboat started filling up with water. Now I realized why the signs were posted there. The paddleboat was leaking. When I told my dad this, his instructions were to peddle faster! Within minutes as we tried to get back to the dock, the boat quickly began to sink, and there was nothing I could do about it. Before I knew it, I was now waist deep in the water. Because I never learned to swim, I started to panic and cry out for help. Within a few minutes (though it seemed like hours) the lifeguard and the boatman rescued us both.

That experience happened over 50 years ago and I still remember it (and relive the pain) as if it were yesterday. Surprisingly enough, how I processed that event, has shaped the way I perceived all other painful events in my life until very recently. The fact that I trusted my father (whether an alcoholic or not) and he put me in harm's way, affected how and if I would ever trust again! This extremely painful incident was the catalyst I used to put up a "pain barrier" or "shield of mistrust" that I would hide behind from that point forward.

In Genesis chapter 2, God showed Adam specific "signs" and boundaries designed to ensure a happy, peaceful and prosperous life.

"The LORD God took the man and put him in the garden of Eden to work it and keep it. And the LORD God commanded the man, saying, "You may surely eat of every tree of the garden, but of the tree of the knowledge of good and evil you shall not eat, for in the day that you eat of it you shall surely die." (Genesis 2:15-17-ESV).

In the verse above, notice the embedded message of love God had for Adam (and for us). These "commands" (specifically designed by God) were to be a part of Adam's blessing. Consider this: God loved him (***providence***). The Latin root of **providential** is providentia, "divine foresight or precaution[3]." God placed Adam where he needed to be at the time he needed to be there. Then God gave Adam a job (***responsibility***). Following this, God made sure that Adam's basic needs were covered (***provision***). God then gave Adam but one boundary (***restriction***) for his own protection, "the tree of the knowledge of good and evil you shall not eat...you will surely die" (***consequence***). After this series of events, we all know the tragic outcome. Adam (and Eve) experienced a painful separation from God that still has far-reaching implications for us today. It doesn't matter who was at fault! Pointing a guilty finger now by no means eases the pain.

I have thought back on my own paddleboat experience and asked several questions. "What if I would have shouted louder to my dad?" "What if I would have just stopped and refused to go forward?" "What if I would have just run away?" Would any of those things have changed the outcome? Possibly! However, I have had 50 years to reach the same conclusion you, my reading friend, must reach regarding your painful situation.

Listen to me, please... the time machine is broken and you must realize that there is no going back! The enemy, no doubt, has been playing mind games with you. I have learned three practical lessons when dealing with my own pain. First, **acknowledge** the hurt (but do not become paralyzed by it). Second, **accept** the current circumstance as rebuilding platform for the future. What lessons can I learn from this that I can use to help me become a better person? Please believe that you will come out of this experience with a stronger faith in our Lord and with the experience, in the future, to walk alongside someone else. Third, **affirm** that no matter what happens from this point forward (like Job) **"I will not charge God with wrong!"** (Job 1:22)

Using this personal "montra,"[4] I have found that no matter how dark my painful experience, the light at the end of the tunnel is reachable and attainable. I'm sure you have heard it said that light exposes darkness. Understandably then, when you look at most New Testament references to Christ and having a relationship with Him, the analogy of light is used. Consider just a few references:

"In the same way, let your light shine before others, so that they may see your good works and give glory to your Father who is in heaven."
Matthew 5:16 (ESV)

"The light shines in the darkness, and the darkness has not overcome it." John 1:5 (ESV)

"Believe in the light while you have the light, so that you may become children of light."
John 12:36 (NIV)

"But you are a chosen race, a royal priesthood, a holy nation, a people for his own possession, that you may proclaim the excellencies of him who called you out of darkness into his marvelous light."1 Peter 2:9 (ESV)

The truth is, nowhere in scripture is it found that we as the people of God should praise God when things are going good. In fact, these dark times should often signal a time of deep reflection, honest self-examination and growth stimulating questions. For us to grow through our pain, we must ask some hard questions. This can be done in the still of your heart between you and God. Questions like:

1. How did I get to this place in my life?
2. Were there signs that I didn't see that got me here?
3. What areas of my life do I need to grow in so that this doesn't happen again?
4. Am I willing to put in the work it takes to grow past this?

For deeper or more detailed answers to these and other questions, please seek the help of a licensed professional counselor. Again, the purpose of this writing is to encourage you through this initial stage of hurt so that you don't become bitter for the rest of your life. I want to encourage you (from the word of God), to push past this pain and move on to become a better person because of this (not in spite of this). The choices you must make from this point forward have to be both deliberate and intentional. Please also understand, my reading friend, right now you may be emotionally vulnerable. Be careful not to make any quick, snap, rash or reactive decisions. To do so at the juncture may have irreversible consequences.

The enemy does some of his best works in the mind. Your task is to make sure that God is glorified and magnified especially in your thoughts. Consider Romans 12:2:

> *"Do not be conformed to this world, but be transformed by the renewal of your mind, that by testing you may discern what is the will of God, what is good and acceptable and perfect." (ESV)*

My reading friend, please do not give up! With every challenge comes change. Think about this quote by Fred Devito, *"If it does not challenge you, it cannot change you."* The truth is, right now with the pain you are facing (or have faced) you have changed (and will continue to change). The question is, "Are you willing to do what it takes to proactively change?" Or are you going to allow this circumstance to cause you to reactively change? The choice is yours.

Chapter Three – Time for Some New Friends

When I was in middle school (back then it was Junior High), I was faced with a new set of challenges and dilemmas. I remember that transition very well. If I had to describe me in elementary school, that person was reserved, compliant and obedient. By the time I went on to Middle School, most of the close friends I attended Elementary with started enrolling in private schools. Looking back now, I can tell you that was a time of painful turmoil. It may have been just normal growing pains but what stands out in my mind are the crystal clear memories of having to choose sides to try and fit in with the new crowd. One of the leaders of this "new crowd" was a boy named Henry Collins. Henry was a natural leader, but his influence guided people in the wrong direction. Unfortunately, I was becoming one of his most devoted followers.

Since our school was only a few minutes' walk from a neighborhood convenience store, One day, Henry had an amazing idea! *"Let's go to the store down the street and get our own lunch! We will be back before anyone knows we were even gone."* Without hesitation or considering the consequence, off we went. My inner voice told me that what we were doing was so wrong. However, I guess I really wanted to fit in with the "cool kid" so bad that I gave no thought about consequences.

We made it to the store and started to head back to school. Although my heart was still racing (not from the fast-paced walk) but from the feeling of guilt that now began to overtake me. *"See Shadow (my middle school nickname), I told you there was absolutely nothing to worry about. We are gonna make it back in no time!"* His words did very little to deal with that sick feeling my stomach was now developing. For an instant, I began to think he might be right. Nevertheless, when we turned the last corner to head back on school grounds, my worst fears would soon come to pass. "Henry, where is everybody?" I asked! "Where are all the kids?" The side of our campus during B lunch (our assigned time) was normally full of people at the picnic tables, laughing, talking and teasing. Instead, there was complete silence. The two of us froze like a proverbial deer in the headlights. Before we could even speak and try to devise an appropriate cover story, we saw Assistant Principal Grimes coming out of the side door. As long as I live, I will never forget her classic response, "I should have known it would be you, Mr. Collins," she said to Henry who already had a recognized presence with the office staff. "But you, Mr. Man (pointing directly to me), I would have never guessed this! You too picked the wrong day to leave campus during lunch!" I forgot that the bags in our hands were a dead giveaway. "That's one of the good things about fire drills during lunch." She explained.

"But, Mrs. Grimes" Henry began to speak... "I don't want to hear it, Mr. Collins," she interrupted. "Head to the office, gentlemen...now please!" With that, the two of us marched to the office like a couple of inmates on death row. Henry seemed unbothered by this turn of events, but to say that I wasn't doing well would be an understatement. Mrs. Grimes took Henry in her office first while my torture was extended by waiting in her outer office. As if the pain of the circumstance wasn't bad enough but to know that the passers-by saw me sitting there through the window didn't make things any better. The additional feelings of guilt, shame and remorse soon joined me on that small narrow bench. "Mr. Man, come in here!" she said as I saw Henry leaving. "Close the door and sit down!" she said. It took all of the strength I could generate to fight back the tears. "Mr. Man," she began, "I have known you since you were in the second grade, sir. I would have never believed you're capable of something like this! Henry says that this whole escapade was your idea! He says he was just following your lead!"

At that instant, I lost it! The tears started to uncontrollably fall, and in my seventh grade already cracking voice I said, *"Mrs. Grimes, you have to believe me! I was following Henry! It was all his idea and not mine!"* as my tears continued to fall. I couldn't believe it. The kid who I thought was cool lied on me! After what seemed like hours, she said to me, *"Mr. Man, look at me! I believe you! Sir, let this be a lesson to you. You are not a little kid anymore. You can make better choices. And Mr. Sir, the way I see it, you need some new friends."* Mrs. Grimes then instructed me to go to the restroom, clean up and go on to my next class.

My reading friend, that incident happened to me over four decades ago and even now, (as I recall the event) my eyes are watering. The lesson that Assistant Principal Grimes taught me was more than just how to make better choices. I have come to realize that God took that situation and gave me a powerful spiritual message.

During the painful episodes of my life, God seemed to refer me back to the Old Testament book of Job. Job was a man who was very wealthy and lost everything in a very short period. However, what is always interesting to me is the friends that Job had. Job's three friends, Eliphaz, Bildad, and Zophar, have historically been known for offering lengthy speeches that resulted in their being condemned by God (Job 42:7–9). At one point, Job, weary of their unhelpful rhetoric, told them, "You are miserable comforters, all of you!" (Job 16:2).[5] It is my opinion, Job's three friends did at least three things right! Consider Job 2:11-13 (ESV):

> **Now when Job's three friends heard of all this evil that had come upon him, they came each from his own place, Eliphaz the Temanite, Bildad the Shuhite, and Zophar the Naamathite. They made an appointment together to come to show him sympathy and comfort him. And when they saw him from a distance, they did not recognize him. And they raised their voices and wept, and they tore their robes and sprinkled dust on their heads toward heaven. And they sat with him on the ground seven days and seven nights, and no one spoke a word to him, for they saw that his suffering was very great.**

First, they came to him when he was suffering. Second, they empathized with him: "they began to weep aloud, and they tore their robes and sprinkled dust on their heads" (verse 12). Third, they spent time with him. Verse 13 states they were with him for seven days before they offered their advice. They spent time with their friend in silence. Later in scripture, we know that God condemned their advice (Job 42:7) but this writer must compliment their actions!

Regarding your pain, my reading friend, like Job, you must be tired of all the well-intended "friends" that have attempted to offer you solace in your situation. Like me, you most likely stopped listening to their "words of wisdom" which in most cases offer little comfort. It occurred to me that if I was going to get any relief, I would first have to get a proper understanding. Solomon recorded on Proverbs 4:7, *"The beginning of wisdom is this: Get wisdom, and whatever you get, get insight."* (ESV).

I began thinking about the family I was born into. My siblings are all different from me but have very similar characteristics. In some families, the siblings possess great athletic abilities. While other families have great artistic or creative abilities. My sisters and I were blessed with a quick "wit" and above-average verbal communication skills. Pain is also a family affair. While I don't know the parents or the birth order of the children, pain to me has two siblings: guilt and shame.

Guilt is a verdict, an awareness of failure against a standard. **Shame is a feeling**, a sense of exposed failure before someone else.[6] In chapter 3 of Genesis, we read of doubt, rebellion and disobedience. We see perfect relationships altered in a seemingly irreparable way. Adam and Eve doubted God's care and goodness toward them, in ways that seem harmless. God charged them as stewards for all that He had created, but for their good put boundaries in place. To protect them. They gave into unhealthy doubt and rebelled against His boundaries
choosing disobedience. From that moment, their relationship with their Creator was
broken – they offended their good and perfect Father.[7]

Imagine for a moment, the feelings associated with that painful incident Adam and Eve must have had. Once they both realized the full magnitude of what happened, I wonder what they talked about? Or how they treated one another? It is certain we don't know. The talks could have been about rejection, blame or brooding. All of these emotional factors are common especially when trying to overcome pain.

Rejection actually activates the same pathways in your brain as physical pain, which is one reason why it hurts so much. The sooner you let go of painful rejections, the better off your mental health will be. When you ruminate, or brood, over a past hurt, the memories you replay in your mind only become increasingly distressing and cause more anger — without providing any new insights. In other words, while reflecting on a painful event can help you to reach an understanding or closure about it, ruminating simply increases your stress levels. Guilt can be beneficial in that it can stop you from doing something that may harm another person (making it a strong "relationship protector"). However, guilt that lingers can impair your ability to focus and enjoy life.[8]

In the case of Adam and Eve, scripture does indicate that they were able to get past the hurt and move on. Genesis 4:1 reads, "Now Adam knew Eve his wife, and she conceived and bore Cain, saying, "I have gotten a man with the help of the LORD." The implication here seems to carry a much more positive tone than we read at the close of Genesis chapter 3. Obviously, some time has passed. The first couple seemingly has moved past that painful experience. They seem to have grown past guilt and now can see past shame. The question is, "How?"

Today, we are still living in the legacy of their guilt. Their doubt, rebellion and disobedience are ours.[9] I would submit that they both refocused on God. Eve's statement at the end of Genesis 4:1 says the blessing came "from the Lord." It seems simple and yet may be so profound. Please understand my point clearly, my reading friend. Our relationship with our Lord does not shield us or make us immune to painful occurrences in our lives. The choices we (and others make) affect us. However, in the case of the first couple, decisions led to sin. Sin separated them from the presence of God. With the passage of time, they were able to grow around guilt, see past shame to recognize and give thanks to God for His blessings! The bottom line is when it comes to painful experiences (no matter how deep), we must embrace them, learn from them and "grow on." If you have made best friends with the family of pain, guilt and shame and have yet to move beyond their initial impact and influence, then, as my Junior High Assistant Principal, Mrs. Grimes, told me, *"It's time for some new friends!"*

Chapter Four -
The Faith to Forgive

Shadow, hurry up! We are going to miss the bus!" Michael yelled inside my house from the front porch. "I'm going as fast as I can!" I yelled back. "Besides, we have plenty of time!" I shouted reassuring him. "You just want to get a seat next to her." I teased. Running out of my front door, I hurriedly said goodbye to my mother and sister. Michael and I then started our run to the bus stop. "This is it, Shadow! First day of High School." Michael was more excited than I was to begin our freshman year.

Michael and I met in Band Camp the summer before 8th Grade. Michael's family just moved down from Atlanta after his dad got a job with the Port Authority. At Band Camp, we were both good at site reading music and the instructors said we both had leadership abilities. I would help the other trumpet players and he would assist the drummers. After we met, we just kind of hit it off. We later discovered that both of us loved to read and each liked Star Trek. At Band Camp, Michael started talking with Michelle (whom I have known since elementary) and he really liked her. Usually, she rode the same bus. That's why he told his mom that he would walk down to my house and catch the bus from there.

Once the bus arrived, Michael was sad to see that Michelle wasn't on the bus. We both learned later that she wouldn't be riding the bus since her older sister started driving. Michael's disappointment was soon replaced by his earlier excitement, as the bus arrived on campus. We got off the bus and headed for the cafeteria. The place was filled with the usual "first day of school" noises. As Michael and I started to walk through the serving line, I stopped in sheer panic! I just froze and couldn't move! "Shadow, man, get going," Michael said as he tried to push me forward. "Man, go! What's the matter with you?" Michael's voice (and all the noise around me) began to fade as though I was going deaf. It was as if for an instant, time stopped. I just kept looking over at the line where you put up your tray and saw him standing there. A little taller and a little older but it was him. He put his tray and walked my direction. It was Henry Collins. The person who lied against me in Middle School. After our off-campus excursion, I took Mrs. Grimes' advice and avoided him ever since. As he got closer, our eyes made contact. He paused briefly and gave me that "acknowledgement nod" we all gave each other back in the early 70's. As he went past, he nodded and said, "What's up" and kept walking. All of a sudden, my temporary deafness left and I heard Michael (and all the sounds) again. "Shadow, man, what's wrong? Are you alright?" "Excuse me. I'm not hungry and I'm going to class," I told Michael as I hurriedly put back my tray and headed to first period. Michael followed me out of the cafeteria and in the lobby area of the school. We sat on one of the benches (as the bell hadn't rang yet) and we still had some time before class. It was there that I told Mike the whole story.

The fact that I managed to avoid Henry for the rest of Middle School only seemed to make our current reunion that much more painful. I felt sick to my stomach at his very sight! For the rest of that day (and the next few weeks), I allowed Henry to dominate my thoughts and dictate my actions. The worse part about all of this was, Henry didn't give me a second thought! The painful truth about my situation could be summed up in one word, "Forgiveness." It wasn't until years later that I was told an analogy that would help me begin the healing process. "I drank the poison, but was waiting for Henry to die." That idiom to me was ridiculously clear. It was ridiculous for a person to drink poison and expect another person to die. Yet it was clear because it explained (on a basic level) why I still had these harsh feelings towards Henry. The truth is that later in High School, Henry got himself into some serious trouble for armed robbery and went to prison. Even hearing that news and feeling the sense of emotional gratitude did little to settle the sick feeling in my stomach at the mere mention of his name. I began to understand the expression that my dad so often used when avoiding people he felt had wronged him, "I don't want to see you, or nobody that looks like you!" To admit the truth, I wanted revenge! I felt I was wronged and I wanted payback. The way I wanted revenge was best said in the movie, *Star Trek II: The Wrath of Khan.* The character Khan (played by Richardo Montalban) said that, "revenge is a dish that is best served cold." Wow! Hearing those words felt so good (when I thought about my situation and other hurts in my life). However, as a Christian believer, I found it very hard to reconcile those harbored feelings with biblical principles. So, I began my quest on the study of forgiveness. To try to find answers on how to get the light of God's word to shine on my dark feelings of hurt, pain and anger.

I do want you to understand, my reading friend, that I am by no means an expert on the subject of forgiveness. I began my quest by desperately asking God for answers (as you must have). I admit that I am still on that quest today. The answers that God has shown me so far, have allowed me to have peace so I can better live with the pain. Yes, there is still pain but it's not as bad as it was. I can now sleep restfully at night. I can now live my life without spending each waking moment replaying the painful video on the YouTube of my mind. One of the first things I needed to do was to get a good definition of exactly what forgiveness is. By definition, forgiveness is the "process of granting pardon for or remission of an offense. To cease to feel resentment against."[10]

That definition was my first starting place. I began to ask myself four questions. First, why did I still feel resentment towards Henry (and others) in my life for something that happened in the past? Second, as a believer in God, how was I going to get to the point where my feelings didn't interfere with my faith? Third, how (as a believer) was I going to give glory to our Lord in my life (with this pain) without being a hypocrite? Fourth, how could I get to the place where I see the "Henrys" in my life, as children of God and not "sub-human soap scum?"

I prayed to God continually and in earnest for a long time. I began to understand that because of my own hurt, I built these walls (invisible boundaries) around me. I originally thought the walls were to keep people out. Keep them away. Keep anyone from getting too close. After all, my trust had been breached once before and for sure wasn't about to consciously make that mistake again! The "Henrys" (the painful places) of my life would have to work hard to either climb over or tunnel under the barricades I constructed.

It was then, my reading friend, that my journey (empowered by God), led me to the next truth. The fact is that walls (or barricades) serve two purposes: not only do they keep things out, but these self-made dividers also keep things in! The unintentional truth, I discovered that I built these stockades to keep in the very pain I was trying find relief for. The undeniable truth was that I not only kept in this pain, but I used it like a comforter on a cold winter night. It insolated me and provided companionship.

I came across two quotes that would kick-start my healing. The latter part of the quote by T.F. Hodge was the first that convicted me. He says that in order to overcome frustration we must "focus on the outcome rather than the obstacle."[11] I found that this applied to me as well when trying to grow around life's challenges. I discovered that I had been so fixated on the obstacle, that I hadn't taken the time to consider the outcome! The second was a quote by Oprah Winfrey regarding forgiveness: She says that, "forgiveness is giving up the hope that the past could have been any different, it's accepting the past for what it was and using this moment and this time to help yourself move forward."[12]

These quotes provided me the answers to my earlier questions. First, I wanted the resentment gone. Second, I most certainly didn't want my feelings to interfere with my faith. Third, I wanted to be able (in the future) to use this experience for the glory of God! Fourth, I wanted the "Henrys" in my life to have the same blessings that God bestows upon me. The first step was to make right a great wrong I had done. By focusing more on the obstacle more than the outcome, I realized there was no room in my heart for anything else. Consider what the bible says in Colossians 1:26, 27:

"the mystery hidden for ages and generations but now revealed to his saints. To them God chose to make known how great among the Gentiles are the riches of the glory of this mystery, which is Christ in you, the hope of glory" (ESV)

I realized that before I could grow forward, I had to take a step back and repent (apologize) to God for the wrong I had done in my heart. To me, it was wrong to ask Him to help me move forward, when I had denied Him in heart. Yes, I still faithfully attended corporate worship. Yes, I still taught my Bible Classes and maintained my other congregational responsibilities. But, in my innermost thoughts, I was wrong. God and I knew it and I proceeded to make it right!

Following that, the scriptures continued to provide me with clarity, comfort and cheer. I now felt like I had fresh eyes to look clearly into the mirror of God's word. I began to think about forgiveness and faith being linked together. If in fact, we as believers are called to be "Christ-like" then it was time to revisit the central point of our faith. Christ and His crucifixion in the gospels now served me as a rallying cry to work even harder to push past this pain.

My wife taught me some profound lessons during the child-bearing years of our marriage. For nine months, I watched her struggle, endure pain and physical changes to her body. She went through the process of labor (three times) and tells me (each time) when the doctor placed that new life on her stomach, pain took a backseat to the joy of our child. Now that our children are adults, we don't talk about the pain of her labor or delivery. We talk about how wonderfully blessed our family is to have raised three God-respecting people! To fully appreciate the events of the crucifixion, it is important to note one of the preluding events, The Garden of Gethsemane. In Matthew 26:39, the scriptures record:

"Then Jesus went with them to a place called Gethsemane, and he said to his disciples, "Sit here, while I go over there and pray." And taking with him Peter and the two sons of Zebedee, he began to be sorrowful and troubled. Then he said to them, "My soul is very sorrowful, even to death; remain here, and watch with me." And going a little farther he fell on his face and prayed, saying, "My Father, if it be possible, let this cup pass from me; nevertheless, not as I will, but as you will."

The "cup" to which Jesus refers is the suffering (pain) He was about to endure. It's as if Jesus was being handed a cup full of bitterness with the expectation that He drinks all of it. Jesus is fully God, but He is also fully human. His human nature, though perfect, still struggled with the need to accept the torture and shame (pain) that awaited Him. In Gethsemane, Jesus conquered the flesh (pain) and kept it in subjection to the spirit. He did this through earnest prayer and intense, willful submission to God's plan.[13]

Now, my reading friend, consider the central point of our Christian faith... the crucifixion. In Luke 23:33-35, reflect on:

"And when they came to the place that is called The Skull, there they crucified him, and the criminals, one on his right and one on his left. And Jesus said, "Father, forgive them, for they know not what they do." And they cast lots to divide his garments. And the people stood by, watching, but the rulers scoffed at him, saying, "He saved others; let him save himself, if he is the Christ of God, his Chosen One!" (ESV)

Here, our Lord was able (even in the midst of pain) to by faith ask forgiveness on the part of the malefactors (in spite of the wrong being done to Him). Our Lord walked the path of the Via Dolorosa (a street in the old city of Jerusalem) on his way to be killed. It is translated "the way of grief" or the "way of sorrow."[14]

My reading friend, let you and I pause for a minute and just talk. I respect and acknowledge your pain! I don't know whether the source of your pain is because you hurt someone or someone hurt you. It really doesn't matter at this point. You and I know that eventually, you are going to have to deal with forgiveness.

Forgiveness is a two-way street. It must be both accepted and given. You may not agree with this right now, but forgiveness is more for you than the other person. If you hold on to the negative emotions associated with not forgiving, those cancer cells will metastasize and ruin you spiritually. My advice is, to accomplish this sooner rather than later. It's not a good idea to allow these negative feelings to "fester." True forgiveness begins with acceptance. You may never have all of your "why" questions answered. The person who wronged you (or you may have wronged) may never come offer an apology. To quote Robert Brault, *"life becomes easier when you learn to accept an apology you never got."*

One of my favorite movies, stars Sidney Poitier and Spencer Tracy. The movie is the classic; *Guess Who's Coming to Dinner.*[15] There is a scene in the movie where Monsignor Ryan (played by Cecil Kellaway) is talking with Matt Drayton outside on the terrace. His friend, Matt, (whom he has known and respected for over 30 years at first) is not very accepting of the idea that his daughter is marrying a man of another race (called a Negro back then). The Monsignor confronts Matt and says, "It's not every day that a man comes face to face with his principles..." To me, that quote is very true and relevant when it comes to times of struggle. It is during those quiet moments, when we are forced to look at our circumstances through the lens of our own beliefs, that the true nature of our own character comes into crystal clear focus.

Forgiveness must also be accepted. It may be time to also accept the harsh reality that you stand in need of forgiving yourself. Although you may not have wronged anyone, you may need to forgive yourself for your part in all of this. During the painful episodes in my life, I have had to come to forgive myself for what I choose to allow the pain to turn me into. I found that I allowed the anger, hostility and bitterness to turn me into a person who was the complete opposite of the real me. My grandmother used two expressions: "it takes two to do the tango" and "if you lie down with dogs, don't get mad at the fleas!"

Now, my reading friend, as you now walk down your own Via Dolorosa, your own "way of grief", by faith draw encouragement from this passage: 1 John 4: 19-21:

> *"We love because he first loved us.*
> *If anyone says, "I love God," and*
> *Hates his brother, he is a liar;*
> *for he who does not love his*
> *brother whom he has seen*
> *cannot love God whom he*

has not seen. And this commandment we have from him: whoever loves God must also love his brother." (ESV)

Chapter Five - Waiting Room – Taking Pain Off Life Support!

Larry! Come quick!" the shout thundered down the hall coming from the girls' bedroom. "Call the ambulance! She is barely breathing!" Stephanie continued to exclaim! Larry turned back from the direction of the source of the yelling to go find his cell phone. "I tried to help her, Mommy!" their youngest daughter said, trying to reassure her mother. "I tried blowing in her mouth like they showed us in school." "You did good, baby girl...this isn't your fault," Stephanie said as she tried to calm her youngest daughter.

Larry quickly dialed 9-1-1 and gave the operator the life essential information. "Help is on the way, Steph," Larry shouted back. Knowing that they only lived minutes from the ambulance dispatch, Larry ran to his room and put on his workout clothes. He also grabbed his wife's workout clothes and T-shirt then ran to the girls' room. "They will be here any minute!" Larry said as he threw the clothes to his wife. By now, they could hear the sirens approaching their house. "Crystal - come here, baby," Larry motioned to his youngest daughter as he took her out of the girls' room. "Some people are coming to help your sister. They will take her to the hospital. Mommy is going to ride with them and I will go a bit later." "I will take you over to Mrs. Petty's house. I want you to be a good girl and stay with her until I come get you." "Alright Daddy," their younger daughter agreed.

The ambulance arrived and Larry opened the door for them and escorted them to the girls' room. The Paramedics began work on Hannah. By now, she was back to breathing on her own, but it was still very erratic. Within a few minutes, they began loading her on the stretcher for transport to the hospital. Stephanie continued to hold her daughter's hand as they went outside and got into the ambulance. "I'll be right there, Steph, as soon as I can," Larry reassured his wife. Afterward, Larry joined his wife at the hospital. Shortly after that, my reading friend, he called me. Larry and I had worked together at the same company for about 11 years. When I first met them, they didn't have any children.

Once I arrived at the hospital, I found Larry just sitting in the Waiting Room. Naturally, he was glad to see me, but I had never seen him this unsettled. "She has had asthma attacks before," he told me. "But never like this!" He further explained that her breathing treatment was almost done and that the hospital was going to keep her a while longer merely for observation. My friend was facing two of the most severe pains (growth opportunities) he ever had to confront; his own doubts and fears.

As we sat in the waiting room, I deliberately just listened. Not the kind of listening people normally do waiting for the chance to interject their point, but I let him drive the conversation and listened for the sake of listening. "For the first time in my life," Larry told me, "I knew that the solution to this problem was totally not up to me or anything I could do. I was afraid and felt helpless!" He went on to describe things from his perspective.

Larry explained that from the moment his wife shouted for him at home, he had to have total faith, trust and reliance on God. He said he called people for help whom he had never met and trusted that they would send help. Once help arrived, he let the strangers into his home and they took his daughter away. Once at the hospital, people were speaking a language he didn't understand all while assuring him they would take good care of his precious daughter. At one point, he and his wife were escorted to this waiting area while further medical tests were being done. Once the testing was complete, they both had some time to visit with their daughter. He said that Stephanie was with their daughter now and he needed some company so he called me.

Larry wasn't particularly a religious person. He did allow his girls to attend VBS at church. He and his wife would visit from time to time, but Larry wasn't what I would call a regular church goer. But, that night at the hospital, Larry's unique perspective about his situation gave me insight on how to handle painful conditions in my life. I began to think that maybe Larry was on to something. Maybe we should be looking at the painful occurrences in life as the medical community does.

From the time you enter the medical arena for services, you are a "patient."[16] By definition, that means a person receiving or registered to receive medical treatment. More interestingly, look at this word "patient" as a noun. It means able to accept or tolerate delays, problems, or suffering without becoming annoyed or anxious.

My reading friend, isn't it remarkable that being patient is the last thing we want to hear or try to accomplish when hurting emotionally? Medically, pain is used as a pointer or an indicator to signal a deeper issue that must be resolved. On the medical front, we are told to "breathe through" pain and "tolerate" it temporarily while the real medical issue is being addressed. The bible also gives this same advice when dealing with our fellowman. Consider Ephesians 4:1-3 (NASB):

"Therefore I, the prisoner of the Lord, implore you to walk in a manner worthy of the calling with which you have been called, with all humility and gentleness, with patience, showing tolerance for one another in love, being diligent to preserve the unity of the Spirit in the bond of peace."

Displaying patience in our lives (regardless of our current situation) is a deliberate and willful attitude. During this time of "character under construction," Peter in scripture reminds us that, "we find favor with God when we bear up under unjust suffering."[17] Consider 1 Peter 2:19 (NASB):

"Servants, be submissive to your masters with all respect, not only to those who are good and gentle, but also to those who are unreasonable. For this finds favor, if for the sake of conscience

toward God a person bears up under sorrows when suffering unjustly."

I hadn't realized that the phrase "bear up under" in the original language carries a medical connotation. One literal meaning is to "undergo."[18]

When I was in my late 20's, I started having pain in the lower left and right side of my mouth. At first, the sensation wasn't too bad. It was more like severe itching accompanied by minor swelling. As time went on, the pain got worse! It caused me major discomfort and severe headaches. When I finally couldn't take the discomfort any longer, I scheduled a visit with the dentist. It didn't take long for him to tell me that I would have to "undergo" (subject myself to) (bear up under) a process called wisdom teeth extraction. At first, I thought it would just be the two teeth on the bottom that would need to be addressed. However, the dentist told me that the X-rays showed him that the third molars on the top did not have enough room in my jaw to come in. Soon, he said, I would experience the same pain in the top of my mouth that I felt on the bottom. So, without hesitation, I submitted. After the in-office procedure, I went home with antibiotics, pain medications and other post-op instructions. The main thing I remember the dental assistant saying was to make sure I "stayed ahead of the pain." I really wasn't quite sure what that meant and did not ask for clarification because I was anxious to get home and go to bed.

Later that evening, after the anesthetic wore off and the pain from the process reasserted itself with a vengeance, I gave my wife the following instructions:

First, bury me in my blue suit rather than the grey one. I realized that I had gained a few pounds and the blue suit looked better on me, I thought. Second, have the choir sing all my favorite hymns at the memorial service. Third, set up a college scholarship fund at church to help the young people with books and other minor expenses! In short, I was ready (and thought I was heading) to be forever with our Lord and His angels!

Seriously, my reading friend, the pain from the procedure, in that moment was far worse than the condition itself. While I was hurting, I could not fathom how I was ever going to heal from this. I had to remember not to let my current condition become my conclusion. It was then that the words of the dental assistant replayed in my mind "stay ahead of the pain." I realized that she meant for me to take the pain meds every four hours as instructed. That way, the medication would already be in my system to combat the pain.

I didn't realize it back then, but that advice works very well on the spiritual front. In order to "stay ahead" of spiritual pain, it is important to understand what you are currently undergoing and try to step back to see a bigger picture. Remember, pain is a pointer. Applying this principal to my dental situation, I could then focus on the benefits of having the procedure (long term healing) rather than my current condition (excessive, excruciating pain). The writer of Hebrews lends some perspective on this. Consider Hebrews 10:35,36 (ESV)

"Therefore do not throw away your confidence, which has a great reward. For you have need of endurance, so that when you have done the will of God you may receive what is promised."

As I began to do some deep internal reflection about how I have handled painful episodes in my life, I had to admit to myself that emotional pain was not the problem. Each time I hurt someone (or I was hurt by someone), the truth is I kept that pain on life support. It consumed my every waking moment and dominated my every conversation. When I was speaking with someone, I couldn't wait to bring my pain into the conversation. This may not have been on a conscious level, but I certainly noticed that it was a pattern. I had to break that pattern if I wanted complete healing and total freedom from that pain. In essence, I came to realize that pain must be **transformed** rather than **transferred**.[19]

The truth is that I had to learn from the mistakes of my past so as not to repeat the same faults in the future. The word, transform, means to change in character or condition. [20] I did not want the pain of my previous regrets transferred to people I love and care about. If left unresolved, there was no way I was going to pull the plug on this pain and allow God to bring in hope and healing. The pain of this circumstance would continue to stay on life support and fester. Maybe like you, my reading friend, that was something I just did not want to happen.

While I was in this spiritual "waiting room," I prayerfully received encouragement from the scriptures in the book of Daniel. I was already familiar with the events of his life, but the book gave me a new perspective when I thought about things from a waiting room perspective. Imagine this "Lion's Den Experience" as a waiting room for Daniel. A place where you have no choice but to totally rely on and trust in God completely. How he got there was not of his own choosing. You would do well to go back and read the book of

Daniel in its entirety. There were three points of encouragement Daniel provided me while he was in his very own "Waiting Room." First, he wasn't willing to compromise his standards (beliefs).[21] Once Daniel was selected to serve in the king's palace, he refused to conform. His body may have been in Babylonian captivity, but his heart was not. Consider Daniel 1:8:

"But Daniel purposed in his heart that he would not defile himself with the portion of the king's delicacies, nor with the wine which he drank; therefore, he requested of the chief of the eunuchs that he might not defile himself."
(New King James Version)

Second, God was the central aspect in the life of Daniel. He already had a right and true relationship with God before hard times came. Consider Daniel 6:4:

"Then the presidents and the satraps sought to find a ground for complaint against Daniel with regard to the kingdom, but they could find no ground for complaint or any fault, because he was faithful, and no error or fault was found in him."

Third, Daniel did not waiver in the midst of hard times. In fact, his convictions grew even stronger when he knew his enemies were deliberately scheming against him. Consider this:

"All the presidents of the kingdom, the prefects and the satraps, the counselors and the governors are agreed that the king should establish an ordinance and enforce an injunction, that whoever makes petition to any god or man for thirty days, except to you, O king, shall be cast into the den of lions. Now, O king, establish the injunction and sign the document, so that it cannot be changed, according to the law of the Medes and the Persians, which cannot be revoked." Therefore, King Darius signed the document and injunction. When Daniel knew that the document had been signed, he went to his house where he had windows in his upper chamber open toward Jerusalem. He got down on his knees three times a day and prayed and gave thanks before his God, as he had done previously." Daniel 6:7-10 (ESV)

My reading friend, with God's help and primary encouragement from the book of Daniel, I was able to grow past the sting of my pain and take that pain off life support. I could now begin to see and understand that in my pain, God had a plan.[22] I was able to "grow on" just as you will. The important fact for me (and you) is the enemy did not win! Consider what Paul said about our Lord:

"But thanks be to God, who gives us the victory through our Lord Jesus Christ. Therefore, my beloved brothers, be steadfast, immovable, always abounding in the work of the Lord, knowing that in the Lord your labor is not in vain." I Corinthians 15:57,58 (ESV)

Chapter Six - From Tears to Cheers – The Storm is Passing Over

J ust as Hurricane Harvey wrapped up its devastation of Houston, Irma got into line behind it and quickly built into the strongest Atlantic hurricane in recorded history. Now, Maria leaves a broken Caribbean in its wake."[23] The hurricane season of 2017 brought many challenges for people affected. However, on a positive note, the devastation and destruction in areas like Houston, Texas, the state of Florida and the island of Puerto Rico provided opportunities to rebuild and for improvement!

There are two expressions, associated with storms, which have always fascinated me. The word, "aftermath" and the phrase, "relief effort." By definition, aftermath is "the period immediately following an unusually ruinous event."[24] The aftermath following a storm or "ruinous" event, is usually a time of cleanup and assessment.

My reading friend, as we approach the end of our journey together, I find interesting parallels that apply to the storms of life as well. In truth, our lives are cyclical with regard to emotional turbulence. It has been said, that at any given time we are at one of three stations concerning life's storms: you are heading for a storm, in the midst of a storm or coming out of a storm. Like me, you may find that you are in the aftermath of your painful storm. For us, this is a time of cleanup and assessment. We must clean up the mess the storm left! Whether or not the storm was your fault isn't the issue right now. The storm has passed (at least the initial effects). We must now begin the process of clean up. You cannot live in the stench, sludge and deluge of your emotional storm no more than you can live in the stench, sludge and deluge from a physical storm. You must take the necessary actions to begin to rebuild. In the physical (and emotional) sense, damaged items must be hauled off. Debris must be picked up. Things that were dirty must be cleaned, salvaged (as much as possible) and sanitized. Only then can you begin to take proper inventory or assessment of what you have left.

I have several friends who work in the insurance industry. They have told me that when people clean up after a disaster, material possessions are looked at in a whole new light. The "little things" in our lives begin to matter a lot more than the larger more physical items. Expensive sound systems, televisions and computers are far less valuable to them than pictures, family keepsakes and other items of more sentimental value. Maybe that perspective is the way we should live our lives on a daily basis. In Luke chapter 12, the scriptures tell us the parable of the Rich Fool. The story is about a man who made the mistake of substituting his "things" (possessions) for life. He failed to realize that once this decision is made, we stop living by faith and trusting God. The words of Jesus in the aftermath of this parable are astonishing. In short, our Lord encourages us not to be anxious:

"And he said to his disciples, "Therefore I tell you, do not be anxious about your life, what you will eat, nor about your body, what you will put on. For life is more than food, and the body more than clothing. Consider the ravens: they neither sow nor reap, they have neither storehouse nor barn, and yet God feeds them. Of how much more value are you than the birds!" (Luke 12:22-24 ESV)

Being anxious is characterized by extreme uneasiness of mind or brooding fear about some contingency. [25] The love that our heavenly Father has for us is not diminished when we are facing tough times in life or when we are very richly blessed. So then, why do we attempt to take matters into our own hands? The foundation of our daily life as believers should continually be faith and trust in Him.

The aftermath following a personal storm is also a good time for evaluation and assessment. No doubt, my reading friend, you have revisited the epicenter of your emotional storm many times in your head already! While you no doubt realize that you cannot go back and undo the past, during this period of cleanup and assessment, I found it helpful to ask myself three vital questions. The answers to these questions would provide some clarity and to ensure that neither fear nor pain legislate our actions. These questions served to anchor me and help me to prepare for the relief efforts that God would soon send my way.

First question, *"Can you identify what you had?"* In other words, prior to the pain of your storm, what were the things that you deemed most important? Maybe it is the good qualities of a broken relationship. Or possibly the precious memories of the loss of a child or loved one. The importance here is to focus on things you can control. During this time of internal reflection, consider encouragement from Galatians 2:20:

"I have been crucified with Christ. It is no longer I who live, but Christ who lives in me. And the life I now live in the flesh I live by faith in the Son of God, who loved me and gave himself for me." (ESV)

Second question, *"What value would you place on what you had?"* For me, my reading friend, this was an important question to ask myself because I had to admit that what I lost seemed more valuable to me after the storm than before. The truth was I took for granted what I had. When I was in college, one of my friends was dating this girl. At the time, those of us around them saw the way he was treating her. Not in an abusive sort of way, but we could tell that his "girlfriend" wasn't a high priority on his list. Once when we were eating in the dining hall, she came over to sit with him. As there were no more chairs, I expected him to make concession (in some way) for her to sit with us. After a moment of her just standing there with the food tray, I got up and offered her my seat. As I was leaving, she very loudly said, "Thank you. It's good to know there are still some gentlemen left in the world!" I looked around, and saw her speaking directly at my friend. It wasn't long before they broke up and she began dating someone else on campus. We could tell that her relationship with this other young man was different. He opened doors for her and saved her a seat at the table. When I asked her later about what was different, she said, "He makes me feel like he wants me!" The second relationship for her was obviously much more valuable than the first. Although, in a marriage context, Ephesians 5:28-30 gives us this encouragement:

"In the same way husbands should love their wives as their own bodies. He who loves his wife loves himself. For no one ever hated his own flesh, but nourishes and cherishes it, just as Christ does the church, because we are members of his body." (ESV)

After identifying what I had, then assigning a value to what I had, the third question almost seemed too simple. The question was, *"Do I want to replace it?"* I again had to make sure that fear and pain didn't answer this question. Remember, my reading friend, before you can receive any "relief efforts" following your storm, this final question completes the assessment. The answer to this question will not only trigger "what was lost in the storm," but it will also point to "how badly do you want to try and replace it." Another way of asking the same question is, "Do you want to put in time and effort to attempt to replace what was lost?"

Realizing that you are currently in the aftermath of your storm allows you to make progress, get ready to receive relief efforts and move on. Coming through your emotional storm means that you have passed through what I call the "Terrible T's." There was a **Transgression** (hurt or pain that either you caused or were affected by). There was a **Termination** (a death and burial). Something died and cannot be retrieved (at least not the way it was). But now you are in **Transition** (resurrection). Consider our Lord when He was on the cross in John 19:28-30:

"After this, Jesus, knowing that all was now finished, said (to fulfill the Scripture), "I thirst." A jar full of sour wine stood there, so they put a sponge full of the sour wine on a hyssop branch and held it to his mouth. When Jesus had received the sour wine, he said, "It is finished," and he bowed his head and gave up his spirit."
(ESV)

Relief effort by definition is a plan to help people and repair damages after a natural disaster.[26] In the case of physical or natural disaster, relief efforts attempt to cover one's basic needs. Notice the case of Jesus in Matthew chapter 4. Here, Christ is growing through His storm as He is being challenged by the devil (the enemy). Interestingly, another name for the enemy here is "slanderer." Once the "slanderer" exhausted every mode of temptation, relief efforts arrived. Consider Matthew 4: 10,11:

"Then Jesus said to him, "Be gone, Satan! For it is written, "'You shall worship the Lord your God and him only shall you serve.'" Then the devil left him, and behold, angels came and were ministering to him." (ESV)

My reading friend, receiving relief efforts is the part of my growth after the storm, that I had the most trouble with. There are good people, divinely motivated, around you that know you are hurting and want to help. You must let them! For sure, there are others who aren't divinely inspired, and just want the sorted details of your pain. You will have to do your best to discern. I have found, that there are far more good people out there than bad. Have you ever noticed that during relief efforts when people bring food and supplies, they don't pass out a menu? That's because right now people are just trying to get you what you need. When you are strong enough and can stand on your own, you can then get what you want.

While you are in this transition, please also know that there is a "new normal." You may have to seek outside (professional) help to make further life changing moves. But, be rest assured, my reading friend, during this time of transition, it is totally up to you to make positive choices. It is important to be certain that you are making the choices and not the pain from the past. Even if the worst of your storm isn't completely over, your attitude and choices going forward will set the stage for how you deal with future challenges. What should be at the forefront of your mind right now is that choices have lifelong consequences. In Deuteronomy, Moses delivers his final words of warning and wisdom to the Israelites before they enter the Promised Land. In chapter 30, he specifically, gives encouragement about making good and wise choices:

"But the word is very near you. It is in your mouth and in your heart, so that you can do it. "See, I have set before you today life and good, death and evil. If you obey the commandments of the LORD your God that I command you today, by loving the LORD your God, by walking in his ways, and by keeping his commandments and his statutes and his rules, then you shall live and multiply, and the LORD your God will bless you in the land that you are entering to take possession of it. But if your heart turns away, and you will not hear, but are drawn away to

worship other gods and serve them..."
(Deuteronomy 30:14-17 ESV)

One good example of how to take something bad and turn it into good is to study the formation of pearls in oysters. A natural pearl begins its life inside an oyster's shell when an intruder, such as a grain of sand or bit of floating food, slips in between one of the two shells of the oyster. In order to protect itself from irritation, the oyster will quickly begin covering the uninvited visitor with layers of nacre — the mineral substance that fashions the mollusk's shells. Layer upon layer of nacre, also known as mother-of-pearl, coat the grain of sand until the iridescent gem is formed.[27] Consider this encouragement from Romans 8:27,28:

"And he who searches hearts knows what is the mind of the Spirit, because the Spirit intercedes for the saints according to the will of God. And we know that for those who love God all things work together for good, for those who are called according to his purpose." (ESV)

My reading friend, the story is told about a young woman who went to her mother and told her about her life and how things were so hard for her. She did not know how she was going to make it and wanted to give up. She was tired of fighting and struggling. It seemed as one problem was solved, a new one arose. Her mother took her to the kitchen. She filled three pots with water and placed each on a high fire. Soon the pots came to boil. In the first, she placed carrots, in the second, she placed eggs, and in the last, she placed ground coffee beans. She let them sit and boil, without saying a word. In about twenty minutes, she turned off the burners. She fished the carrots out and placed them in a bowl. She pulled the eggs out and placed them in a bowl. Then she ladled the coffee out and placed it in a bowl. Turning to her daughter, she asked, "Tell me what you see." "Carrots, eggs, and coffee," she replied.

Her mother brought her closer and asked her to feel the carrots. She did and noted that they were soft. The mother then asked the daughter to take an egg and break it. After pulling off the shell, she observed the hard-boiled egg. Finally, the mother asked the daughter to sip the coffee. The daughter smiled, as she tasted its rich aroma, the daughter then asked, "What does it mean, Mother?"[28] Her mother explained that each of these objects had faced the same adversity: boiling water. Each reacted differently. The **carrot** went in strong, hard and unrelenting. However, after being subjected to the boiling water, it softened and became weak. The **egg** had been fragile. Its thin outer shell had protected its liquid interior, but after sitting through the boiling water, its insides became hardened. The ground **coffee** beans were unique, however. After they were in the boiling water, they had changed the water. "Which are you?" she asked her daughter. The same question, my reading friend, is for you!

Acknowledgement:

This devotional book is written to everyone

Who has ever felt like giving up and didn't!

Special thanks to my wife Tanjena who watched

me struggle at times and prayed me through!

Next devotional book coming soon:

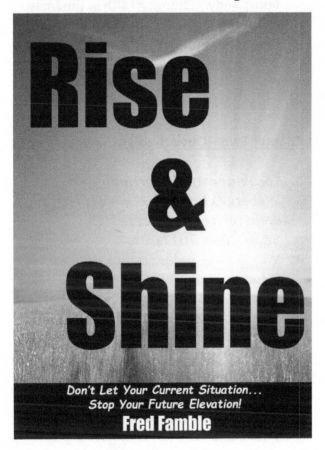

Rise
&
Shine

Don't Let Your Current Situation...
Stop Your Future Elevation!

Fred Famble

End Notes

Chapter One – You Are Not Alone

1. SparkNotes Editors. (2002). SparkNote on Bible: The Old Testament. Retrieved September 10, 2017, from www.sparknotes.com/lit/oldtestament/
2. Cook, Andy. "Choosing Faith in the Midst of Suffering, Job 1-2." LifeWay Christian Resources. Retrieved September 12, 2017, from www.lifeway.com/Article/sermon-choosing-faith-suffering-job

Chapter Two – Obey the Signs

3. "providential." *Merriam-Webster.com*. 2017. www.merriam-webster.com (Accessed 13 September 2017).
4. Wikipedia contributors. "Montra." *Wikipedia, The Free Encyclopedia*. Wikipedia, The Free Encyclopedia, 26 Jul. 2017. Web. 1 Dec. 2017.

Chapter Three – Time for Some New Friends

5. *"What did Job's Three Friends Have Wrong and What did they have right?"*

Web. 15 September 2017.
www.gotquestions.org/Jobs-friends.html

6. "Guilt and Shame: The Elephant in the Room". Shades Montain Baptist Church. Web. 08 February 2015.
www.shades.org/assets/img/uploads/sermons/guilt-shame/downloads/GuiltShame_Sermon_1.pdf

7. "Guilt and Shame: The Elephant in the Room". Shades Montain Baptist Church. Web. 08 February 2015.
www.shades.org/assets/img/uploads/sermons/guilt-shame/downloads/GuiltShame_Sermon_1.pdf

8. Joseph Mercola."Five Tips for Recovering from Emotional Pain." Web. 08 August 2015.
articles.mercola.com/sites/articles/archive/2013/08/15/emotional-pain-recovery-tips.aspx

9. "Guilt and Shame: The Elephant in the Room". Shades Montain Baptist Church. Web. 08 February 2015.
www.shades.org/assets/img/uploads/sermons/guilt-shame/downloads/GuiltShame_Sermon_1.pdf

Chapter Four – The Faith to Forgive

10. "forgive." *Dictionary.com*. 2017. www.dictionary.com (13 September 2017).
11. Hodge, T.F. - From Within I Rise Quotes. August 2017. www.goodreads.com/quotes/455710-to-conquer-frustration-one-must-remain-intensely-focused-on-the

12. Winfrey, Oprah. Quote. August 2017. www.goodreads.com/quotes/376558-forgiveness-is-giving-up-the-hope-that-the-past-could
13. Web Article: "Why did Jesus Ask Let This Cup Pass From Me". gotquestions.org/let-this-cup-pass-from-me.html
14. Wikipedia contributors. "Via_Dolorosa." *Wikipedia, The Free Encyclopedia*. Wikipedia, The Free Encyclopedia, 26 Jul. 2017. Web. Accessed September 2017.
15. Wikipedia contributors. "Guess Who's Coming to Dinner." *Wikipedia, The Free Encyclopedia*. Wikipedia, The Free Encyclopedia, 26 Jul. 2017. Web. Accessed October 2017.

Chapter Five - Waiting Room-Taking Pain Off Life Support

16. Malatt. Anne. "Why are Patients Called Patients". Article: The Doctors Perspective. April 5, 2015. medicineandsergebenhayon.com/2015/04/05/why-are-patients-called-patients/

17. McNab, Allen. "Bible Study.org".Bible Study on Patience. www.biblestudyguide.org/articles/patience/endure-with-much-patience.htm

18. Online Greek Bible. www.messie2vie.fr/bible/strongs/strong-greek-G5278-hypomeno.html Accessed October 2017.

19. Hopler, Whitney. Article: "How to Overcome Past Pain and Let Hope into Your Life". Crosswalk.com. Published October 25, 2013. www.crosswalk.com/faith/spiritual-life/how-to-overcome-past-pain-and-let-hope-into-your-life.html

20. "transform." *Merriam-Webster.com*. 2017. www.merriam-webster.com (Accessed 15 October 2017).

21. Harrub, Will. "Four Lessons from Daniel for Today's Christian". Focus Press. August 2015. www.focuspress.org/2015/08/24/4-lessons-from-daniel-for-todays-christians/

22. Franklin, Kirk. Lyrics to the Song "I Am". www.azlyrics.com/lyrics/kirkfranklin/iam.html

Chapter Six-From Tears to Cheers - The Storm is Passing Over

23. Greshko, Michael. "Why This Hurricane Season Has Been So Catastrophic". News.National Geographic. September 2017. news.nationalgeographic.com/2017/09/hurricane-irma-harvey-season-climate-change-weather/

24. "aftermath." *Merriam-Webster.com*. 2017. www.merriam-webster.com (Accessed 20 October 2017).

25. "anxious." *Merriam-Webster.com*. 2017. www.merriam-webster.com (Accessed 15 October 2017).

26. "relief effort." Englishbaby.com. 2017 www.englishbaby.com/vocab/word/7184/relief-effort

27. Bryner. Michelle. "How Do Oysters Make Pearls". Life Science Online. November 2012. www.livescience.com/32289-how-do-oysters-make-pearls.html

28. Talavera, Karen. "Carrot, Egg or Coffee: Which Are You?". Published January 2012. www.huffingtonpost.com/karen-talavera/carrot-coffee-egg-parable_b_1107628.html

Made in the USA
Monee, IL
14 March 2021

62792376R00049